Walking
in
Sunshine Again

Walking
in
Sunshine Again

Karl Jett
Illustrated by Brynna Golden

XULON PRESS

Xulon Press
2301 Lucien Way #415
Maitland, FL 32751
407.339.4217
www.xulonpress.com

ISBN-13: 978-1-6628-1814-1
Hardcover ISBN-13: 978-1-6628-1815-8
Ebook ISBN-13: 978-1-6628-1816-5

Dedication

To Pumpkin: We both stood and fought this cancer battle together for thirty months. Your strong faith and determination never faltered to the end. Our prayer and scripture-sharing time meant so much to me, and I hold onto dearly our precious memories that we shared together. Words can never express the grief I felt or the stream of tears that flowed from my heart. The comfort I have today is knowing that in your heavenly home, you do not suffer in pain anymore.

Table of Contents

Illustrations

A very special thanks to my granddaughter, Brynna Golden, for helping me tell my story through her awesome illustrations. It was a joy watching her take notes of my descriptions and ideas about the things that I wanted her to draw. She drew all of these illustrations between the ages of eleven and fifteen.

Acknowledgements

I would like to honor these three beautiful women in my life for their contributions to my book. Rachael Jett, my daughter-in-law, had the hard job of transcribing my handwritten notes into a digital format. Janée Golden, my youngest daughter, whose awesome gift in organizing and editing helped form my words into a manuscript. Kareece McKie, my middle daughter, was the final pair of eyes to study my book draft and made the necessary changes to tie everything together. I am very grateful for all the work they provided to help me tell the stories of my life experiences on the farm. I love each one of you dearly.

Introduction

"Howdy, partners!" I have always spoken these two words in greeting each of my five wonderful grandchildren from the time they were little toddlers to the present. I would like to share with you, partners, my story that began the moment I received a grim cancer diagnosis in May of 2011. My Savior began to show and to teach me how the Holy Spirit would lead me by faith and not by sight. Two powerful scriptures, both found in 2 Corinthians, provided me hope and strength to face the obstacles that loomed on the horizon. 2 Corinthians 4:18 tells us, "While we look not at the things which are seen, but at the things which are not seen: for the things which are seen are temporal; but the things which are not seen are eternal." The other key verse found in 2 Corinthians 5:7 states, "For we walk by faith, not by sight."

The amazing travels I have been on, at times, turned into some of the toughest trails. Two of which are when I lost my oldest daughter, Cherinda (who I call Pumpkin), and then a few years later, the passing of my mother, Ramona. In spite of these huge losses, I have been caught up and walked with my Savior in the spiritual realm. I have seen visions and felt His presence, which always brings comfort, peace, and glory.

The following chapters will consist of my day-to-day life experiences on the farm. I will also share three visions that occurred during this time of healing, along with some very powerful scriptures that brought me the strength to fight cancer. Many beautiful gospel songs have been written and recorded throughout the ages. It's very difficult for me to pick a favorite, but there are two in particular that helped define who I am and were great inspiration to me during my journey. I will share the lyrics with you.

Today, my prayer for each of you, as we explore these chapters together, is that you will find that place called heaven and that you will always remember just how much our Father unconditionally loves you. Our mission as Christians is to become sanctified and go into this world as His disciples to testify of His holy Word. These past ten years, I have been reminded over and over again of just how much our Father in heaven loves me. We all have sinned and fallen short on our life's journey, but our Savior is always there to pick up the broken pieces. Through our Father's grace, if we confess our sins to Him, we will be forgiven.

I have been granted an extra chapter to add to my life and, through this process, a burning desire to fulfill it. My purpose has been revealed as I serve Him daily. So, partners, today as you read my story, I challenge each of you to find the purpose that our Father has prepared for you and to live your dreams to the fullest. Your reward will be great!

CHAPTER 1

Posse

My property lies in that thirty-four-mile-wide by one-hundred-sixty-seven-mile-long strip of land where the buffalo once roamed. It was home to the nomadic Native American Indian tribes of the High Plains and was controlled by the Comanche Indians. This strip of land has a very interesting and unique history. Texas borders it on the south at the 36°30′ parallel, New Mexico is on the 103rd meridian along the western border, and Colorado and Kansas form the northern border at the 37th parallel. The remainder of Oklahoma lies at the 100th meridian to the east of this area. In 1819, the Adams-Onis Treaty signed by the United States and Spain formed the western boundary along the 100th meridian. When the Missouri Compromise prohibited slavery north of the 36°30′ parallel and Texas joined the Union on December 29, 1845, this tiny strip of land was left out. In 1854, the Kansas-Nebraska Act was signed, which set the southern border of Kansas Territory along the 37° parallel. When Kansas joined the Union as a state on January 29, 1861, the southern boundary remained the same. As this long strip of land was not part of any state or territory, it became known simply as "No Man's Land." The Panhandle remained unassigned to any state or governance until 1890, when the Organic Act was passed, which assigned this strip of land to the Oklahoma Territory.

Because there were no laws in this strip of land, it became a haven for bootleggers, horse thieves, and cattle rustlers. Only the most rugged and gritty individuals chose to live on this land. These early settlers lived in sod homes and formed vigilante communities for protection and to help maintain law and order. A few men would be sworn in as the small town's sheriff, and at different times, that sheriff would deputize a few honest citizens to help him go after outlaws, gangs, or thieves. This group of lawmen would become known as a posse, and they would not stop until justice was served.

Just like the posse members that once saddled up their horses and rode with true grit and determination to get the outlaws and bring justice, no matter what it took, my posse saddled up with prayers and zeal. They were determined to destroy Satan's attempt to steal my health. It wasn't long before he discovered that with this posse, he couldn't hide nor outrun this resolute bunch.

To those of you who haven't faced a battle with your life hanging in the balance, I will share some insight into the little things that helped carry me through some of the darkest times. And to those of you who have had similar battles, you already understand the importance of encouraging words. The compassion from my church family, relatives, friends, and those I didn't even know, meant so much. Countless prayers, letters, texts, and phone calls encouraged me daily during the battle.

I want to tell you about just a few of these posse members who saddled up and rode with me. Without mentioning any names, they will know who they are. I recall the renewed hope waiting in the mailbox for me each Tuesday at noon—a post card from the Buffalo United Methodist Adult Sunday School Class signed with all the member's signatures, letting me know that they prayed for me that week. This Sunday school class stood beside me, calling out for supernatural healing. I will never forget you all. I pray continued blessings for this special ministry that you have been called to do.

Another posse member, a very precious sister-in-law, has lifted me up by texting scriptures since the beginning and has continued encouraging me for the past ten years. I treasure each of the nearly 300 messages she has sent. She has taught me what a true and faithful servant for Christ really is.

One of my posse members was my late brother-in-law who was literally a giant of a man with a heart of gold. He called me nearly every day from his cell phone. When I answered, his voice always boomed, "Hello, my friend." He wanted to know exactly what was happening in my world each day. He gave me so much hope and always assured me that everything would be OK. He kept encouraging me to give my testimony until he finally said, "Karl, it is time to hear your testimony."

For the next three days, I wrestled with God, asking, "How can I give my testimony? I still have cancer." The fourth morning, I called and said, "Yes, I'm ready." The following month in Woodward, Oklahoma, at the New Covenant men's breakfast, I got up and shared my testimony with this group of Christian men. I would return several times to witness and share the Word of God to my new group of brothers in Christ.

Another posse member is a young woman with a smile and laugh that is so genuine and contagious. She generously gave one of her own kidneys for another man to live and enjoy life again. She is a very giving person who, from day one, wanted to join the posse as a prayer warrior. Another was from Chicago, a tiny great-grandmotherly type with a zeal for life who always prayed bold prayers. True friends come in all ages.

A tiny gal from eastern Oklahoma came to Beaver County and worked in the Natural Resources Conservation Service office for a time. Her eyes always light up when she smiles. She is one amazing lady who has overcome many obstacles in her own life. We were at the office when I received the news that my daughter, Cherinda, had passed away. I was grateful to have her by my side at that very moment. She immediately drove me home and offered comfort to Charlene and me.

A truly amazing lady lived west of Slapout for a time and worked at the Slapout station for several years. She is witty and always smiling, and we became very good friends with her and her family. She knew of the seriousness of the cancer diagnosis when my report came back. Unshaken, she said, "I believe in miracles, and we will beat this. I'm joining your team."

There is a special couple that have been longtime friends of mine who live southeast of Slapout. Both of them kept my hopes up. The husband and I have built many miles of fence together through the years. He would always call and let me know that if there was anything he could do to help, I could count on him. His wife is a very giving, Christian woman who leads our praise and worship during Sunday night service. They are very active in the church, and I value their friendship very much. I am so grateful to them for being there when I needed them most.

Finally, this couple lives a short distance northwest of Slapout and the young woman mentioned earlier is her daughter. They are awesome neighbors and friends that you can call anytime. Several times, we shed many tears at their kitchen table, not tears of sadness but tears of joy as we prayed and shared what was on each of our hearts. They really took Charlene and me under their wings when both Cherinda and I were fighting cancer together. When the clouds were the darkest, they extended their hands and said, "Here we are." And when Cherinda passed away, this dear lady came to our house immediately to be by our side. She is a woman of tremendous faith with a gift of helping others and a willingness and burning desire to serve God. Her husband is a Christian brother who is willing to walk that extra mile with anyone who has a need. He is also an avid deer hunter. Just one peek inside his pickup will reveal that he is armed, because resting on his dashboard next to the steering wheel is his Bible. A strong bond of friendship was formed during this challenging time that Charlene and I faced. Thanks so much for your kindness. We will always be indebted to the both of you.

Last but not least, to my family—Ryan and wife Rachael, their son Justin; Janée and husband Dan, along with Aidan and Brynna; Kareece and husband Derek, along with Tyce and Kade; and to Channing—thanks for your loving support each step of the way. To all my awesome Jett cousins and their families, thank you for your strong Christian foundations and constant prayers that aided in my healing. To all my Bowers brothers-in-law and sisters-in-law and all my nieces and nephews, thanks for always praying the fervent prayers; they really worked. To my only aunt on the Merett side of the family, you have always been such a blessing. Always know that I treasure each of you and I have truly been blessed to be a part of your families.

To my wife, Charlene, the caregiver of all caregivers, your gift to take my pain away, your spirit to lift me up when I needed it, your beautiful prayers for healing, your love and devotion when I felt all alone, your vows for better or worse, thank you from the bottom of my heart. With all my love, Karl.

Today, my prayer for each of you who prayed for my recovery is that the blessings of God will always flow your way and that the floodgates of heaven will open up and pour out to each one of you His riches in glory. Thanks so much for enforcing the words found in the scriptures of God's healing power; we all witnessed His divine intervention in my life. Amen.

CHAPTER 2

Circle the Wagons

My story begins at the age of sixty-one, when I was diagnosed with renal cell kidney cancer in my left kidney that then spread to both lungs and into my brain. My life changed dramatically in May of 2011. One day, I was celebrating the honor of becoming the Area 1 Commissioner for the Oklahoma Conservation Commission. The next day, I received the dreadful report that I had kidney cancer. The elation of being selected by Governor Mary Fallin to serve a five-year term as Area 1 Commissioner turned to utter disbelief that I now had cancer. My initial thought was to call the governor's office to tell them that I needed to back out of this commitment. After much thought and prayer, the next day, I decided that I would serve my term and fight this cancer battle head on.

My initial symptom happened while visiting my daughter, Kareece, and her family in Texas. One night during my stay, I urinated pure blood. The next morning, there was just a trace and nothing ever again. A few days after arriving back in Oklahoma, I traveled to the Laverne Family Health Clinic and visited with my PA, Steve Madrid. He listened intently as I described that I must have passed a kidney stone with no pain whatsoever. Not once did he interrupt as I explained everything to him. After I finished, he simply said he was setting up an appointment for me the following morning at the Harper County Community Hospital in Buffalo, Oklahoma, for a CT scan. The results of this scan soon set up a series of doctor visits to decide who was to perform surgery on the diseased kidney. Finally, the decision led me to Mercy Hospital in Oklahoma City, where Dr. Brian Link performed the surgery.

After removing my left kidney, it appeared that the cancer had been contained within that kidney. But, a chest scan at my three-month checkup revealed much more shocking news. The cancer had spread to my lungs, filling both of them with nodules too numerous to count. There was nothing more Dr. Link could do for me. Dr. Jess Armor, an oncologist, took over my treatments. Sitting there in his office, he began to explain that I had Stage IV kidney cancer, which meant chemo pills to try to buy me a little extra time to live. Dr. Armor explained that I had probably one year to live. But, with all the new, experimental chemo pills, we might be able to extend my life expectancy for three or four more years.

After driving home that night, I went downstairs and prayed, "God, please open my Bible and show me the scriptures I need right now." Then, taking my Bible and placing it before me, I held it until the pages parted to Matthew 9:20–22. These verses tell of the woman who had blood issues for twelve years and came to Jesus when He was preaching to a large gathering. She was at the back and managed to push through the crowd and touch His garments. Her faith told her that if she could just touch His garments, she would be healed. This woman had such incredible faith, and I wanted this same faith. These scriptures helped me so much through a few tough years.

About one month after receiving the grim news of lung cancer, I was sitting at the kitchen table talking to Charlene, when I suddenly felt pain hit me like a sledge hammer underneath my left shoulder. It was unbearable. I struggled to make it to the living room before I collapsed to the floor. Fighting to catch a breath of air, I yelled for help. Charlene managed to get me to the sofa. As I tried to relax, the horrendous pain in my back begin to subside. I laid there motionless, too scared to even move a single finger or toe. Soon, the ambulance arrived for my trip to the Harper County Community Hospital. Waiting for me in the emergency room was my PA, Steve Madrid. After checking me out and finding all my vital signs normal, he suspected I had suffered a seizure. Steve sent me back home, but he scheduled an MRI at the Woodward Regional Hospital for early the next morning in order to find out what had caused the seizure. The results of the MRI revealed that tumors had taken hold in my brain. There were four in total that were removed on my birthday, December 1, 2011, by gamma knife radiation surgery performed by Dr. Reynolds and Dr. Morrison. High doses of radiation were pinpointed directly at the tumors to kill them. In total, the number of brain tumors reached seven before things began to turn around in my favor.

Because the cancer had started in my kidney, then moved to my lungs and brain, I was unable to get into any cancer trials or studies. Over the next three years, I tried several different types of chemo pills without much success, all while fighting side effects like loss of appetite, bouts of diarrhea, tired legs, and intense mouth sores. None of these pills made any improvements in shrinking the tumors in my lungs. One night, the Holy Spirit revealed to me that it was time to quit taking the chemo pills. I prayed earnestly for Him to please send me confirmation if this was indeed to happen.

Early the very next morning, one of my closest prayer warriors called me and said, "Karl, don't you think that it is time to throw your chemo cancer pills away?" She had received confirmation the same night I did. The rest is history. We let our oncologist know that we had thrown the chemo pills in the trash. Very soon after this, the CT scans on my chest and the MRIs on my brain started showing marked improvements. Within the next couple of years, the numerous cancer nodules in both lungs had vanished. Now the scans show a little scar tissue in my lungs and brain where the tumors once thrived. A mighty miracle had happened, which my team of doctors at Mercy Hospital in Oklahoma City witnessed. All the prayers lifted by my prayer warriors were heard in the courts of heaven, and I was healed from cancer. The battle had been won!

Thanks again to my PA, Steve Madrid; my surgeon, Dr. Brian Link; my oncologist, Dr. Jess Armor; my neurosurgeon, Dr. William Emery Reynolds; and my radiologist, Dr. Astrid Morrison. They all believed in me and always helped to keep my spirits high. Each one of them is a highly skilled professional who assisted in stabilizing my body while everything that was about to unfold rested in the hands of God.

CHAPTER 3

Papa's Angels

I t was time for my three-month check-up following the removal of my kidney due to cancer. During this visit, they ran scans on my lungs. The doctor came back into the room to deliver the bad report that the kidney cancer had not been contained. It had spread to both lungs, which were now full of cancer nodules. His words, "There is nothing more I can do," pierced my ears, and my mind drifted back to when I was ten and my granddad Joel Henderson Jett passed away. I remembered the devastation I felt as my tears flowed with his passing. Immediately, my mind went to my five grandchildren, whose ages at that time ranged from three to seven. Sitting there, I uttered a short prayer: "God, please let me get to watch them grow up." This was my deepest desire and something that my granddad Jett didn't get to witness with his own grandchildren.

Three months later on Thanksgiving, in 2011, my oldest daughter Cherinda and I were sitting at the kitchen table of my youngest daughter Janée's house. We both discussed our battle plans for our cancer and what our purpose was moving forward in our lives. Each of the grandkids had been given the chance

13

to draw a few letters of the alphabet on tiny slips of paper that we shuffled together in the hopes that they would form a word. When we placed all the letters together, we were amazed that the letters did form a word: Papa's Angels. Next, we searched for a fitting scripture to go with Papa's Angels and found Proverbs 22:9 (NLT): "Blessed are those who are generous, because they feed the poor." Soon after that day, my purpose was revealed to me—I needed to serve others by becoming a better servant.

Thinking back to my teenage years, it seemed that all my battles were settled either on the football gridiron or on the baseball field. This battle with cancer certainly did not come with all the dugout chatter or the football huddles between each play. First of all, there were no set rules, timeouts, or out-of-bounds calls. This cancer battle was very real, and my body and mind worked overtime day after day for almost four years, until a miracle appeared and all those cancer cells were cast from my body. I did have something very special on my side, though: five little faces watching and cheering as they rooted for me each step of the way. This team of five helped coach and motivate me to victory against some really incredible odds.

It's hard to find the right words to describe the incredible feelings and to measure the amount of love in my heart for each one of my grandchildren. As little children, they all needed me as "Papa," and it has been my honor to be able to watch them grow up to become four awesome young men and one amazing young woman. They all helped to fuel that burning desire from deep within my soul to live for them. Never did fear or even death occur in my mind. Each one of them helped create that deep river of hope that flowed within my body during the hardest days. All of them are truly a gift from heaven, and they brought me untold joy during the bout with cancer. Let me share just a glimpse about each one of them and the things we have shared together.

Kade McKie: Each time Charlene and I traveled to Waxahachie, Texas, Kade stood there by the mailbox waiting to greet us. One trip when he was still just a little fella, he and I were sitting together on a bench outside a restaurant in Arlington, Texas. He knew that we were about to head back home to Oklahoma. He looked squarely into my eyes, and with tears flowing, he said, "Papa, I'm really going to miss you. Please don't go." Time stood still for a few moments as I squeezed his little hand and assured him that it was okay, that I loved him dearly, and that we would see each other soon. That scene became etched in my mind over and over during my cancer battle and helped sustain me during the toughest times of adversity.

A few years later at a little league baseball game, he hit a ball that rolled to the center field fence. Even though Kade was not the fastest runner on the team, I saw the determination on his face as he rounded second. I could tell that no matter where the ball was thrown, he was not going to stop at third. Sure enough, after reaching third base, he rounded it and headed to home plate at full steam. What a moment that was as he crossed home plate for a home run! He used every ounce of his body to make me a proud Papa. As an eighth grader, he played football and crushed his opponents. Now, he is grown up and is also gifted in music. He plays trombone in the Waxahachie marching band and has received All Region Honors for the last two years. The thing that really stands out to me is his infectious smile and outgoing attitude that makes it a pleasure to hang out with him. This past summer, he came to spend a week on the farm. As we worked together, I was amazed at how much he has matured over these past ten years. If just one word was used to describe the trait that he possesses, it would be *loyalty*.

Aidan Golden: I have so many fond memories of him on the farm. My favorite times were spent with him on my tractor out in the field, tilling the soil. The air conditioner, with its cool air blowing on his face, would always put him to sleep as he sat next to me. He has a farmer's mind that he must have inherited from me. As a youngster, he played an online farming simulator game where he would plant certain crops using different options and farming practices to see how much money he could make. I don't ever recall him losing money. Maybe I should let him manage my farm! In real life, a lot more farming challenges arise that are not found in a game.

The first time Aidan got to drive a real tractor was when he was around nine years old, and he drove our small John Deere down the road. I might add that there are highline poles along the north side of the road that are really close to the edge. His eyes were mostly fixed on the back tires as he drove, so the tractor would drift closer and closer to the poles. This caused some very anxious moments for Charlene and me as we followed him. Just as the front tires would hit the rough edge of the ditch, he would glance up at the road and correct his steering back to the middle of the road. This happened several times during the long mile stretch.

Just this past summer, Aidan was on the same small John Deere tractor busily running the front-end loader, loading sand and smoothing it out for a large pad for a twenty-foot stock tank. While watching him operate the tractor with such ease, my thoughts drifted back to that first time he drove this tractor, watching the tires spin. He has grown up from a little boy to a teenager. It has been a privilege to watch him mature into such an awesome young man. As a young teenager, his ambitions shifted from being a farmer to becoming an Air Force pilot, so he joined the Civil Air Patrol. He enjoys playing the trombone and recently traveled through seven countries in Europe, performing concerts as part of the Oklahoma Ambassadors of Music. He is also running cross country and track in high school as a junior. I have no doubt that whatever he decides to do and put his mind to, he will accomplish it. The one word to describe the trait that he possesses is *confidence*.

Brynna Golden: My only granddaughter is a beautiful blue-eyed blonde with lots of class combined with a touch of sass, making this tiny, little girl really full of spunk. When she was running around the house and playing, you would never know when she was going to stop in her tracks and glance at you while holding her two little fingers near her eyes then pointing at you as if to say, "I'm watching you, Papa." On a trip to Boot Hill in Dodge City, Kansas, we got to see the reenactment of the rugged history of the town. The saloon, museum, and the Boot Hill graveyard are all on display for the tourists, along with staged gunfights. While taking in this action, my little beauty put her two fingers up to her eyes and then pointed to one of the gunslingers after the gunfight. Out of the entire crowd, this little girl had captured his full attention. Throughout the next several hours as their paths crossed, whenever he caught her looking his way, he would take his two fingers and hold them up to his eyes and then would point to her as if to say, "I'm watching you too!" It was comical to watch my little granddaughter exchanging pointed fingers back and forth with this scruffy gunslinger. I'm certain that never in all his days of working at Boot Hill in Dodge City had he ever run across anything like my little Brynna.

Throughout the years, I have never seen her without a note pad and a pen, pencil, or crayon drawing something. Now, as a teenager, she has been blessed with the God-given talent as a gifted artist, just like her Aunt Sissy. Her illustrations represent each one of my chapters, capturing scenes that flow to my words. In addition to being a gifted freshman honors student in high school, she is also an excellent cook. Many times when we are together, she fixes breakfast for the whole clan. She has inherited my mom's skill at making pies and most any other dessert. The most famous masterpiece in the history of painting is the Mona Lisa by Leonardo da Vinci, and although I don't know which path my granddaughter will take, if it is painting, just maybe another masterpiece to rival da Vinci's could be in the works. There are two words that it takes to describe her— *imaginative* and *artistic*.

Justin Jett: My youngest grandchild is a very intelligent student along with being a skilled dancer in dance recitals and is part of the robotics team in 4-H. When he was still a little tyke, he would work alongside his dad and mom with tools, trying to help out. Once I remember as his dad was hanging gates on a new fence, Justin was just as busy working behind his dad's back, tying up the gate to the welding trailer with a rope. After his dad was finished, he drove off with the welding trailer. I will just say the results weren't good, but I have to admit Justin's tying up skills were pretty amazing at such a young age. His dad didn't pull the gate from the hinges, but it sure got bent as the welding trailer pulled away.

We have spent many summers together hauling round bales from the field and feeding my cattle on occasion. Once when he was about four years old, as we were headed home from feeding cattle, he glanced over and looked at me and said, "Papa, I really need you." These tender moments are what makes living this life so special. It reminded me of how much I looked up to both my granddads. Another time, my leg was really hurting, and I

18

was limping after getting out of the pickup. Without uttering a word, Justin came around the pickup, took my arm, and placed it over his shoulder. He then said to me, "Papa, you can always lean on me." I never have forgotten this moment.

Justin and I have spent the past several summers working together to dig up musk thistles, which are noxious weeds that have invaded most areas of western and central Oklahoma. It is an invasive species that has lots of thorns and thrives in our crop fields and in the low-lying areas of our pastures. We have shared the task of digging up these plants with shovels. It is not an easy job, as it requires lots of bending and pulling up the weeds by their roots. Justin is a very hard worker and has developed a keen eye for identifying these plants as they sprout. Together, we have dug up these thistles by the thousands.

When we are tagging or banding kid goats, there is nobody as good at catching them by hand as Justin. His reflexes are amazing because he is quick and has catlike moves. I almost can guarantee that if anyone could catch a kid goat in a forty-acre field, it would be Justin. Now, as a seventh grader, he has started running cross country. The one word to describe his personal trait would be *compassion*.

Tyce McKie: My oldest grandchild. We have always shared a love of baseball. At a very young age, his passion was playing baseball. Every time I watched him play, it took me back to my younger years on the baseball diamond. His pitching skills, along with hitting, were way above average. Once in a little league game in Waxahachie, I watched him throw a no-hitter where every out was a strikeout. His performance on the mound that night was incredible. He combined a few fastballs with mostly sliders. His fastball was used to get ahead in the count with the batters, and his sliders that night were unhittable. Those sliders were knee high on the outside corner of the plate. If the batter swung, the pitch dipped with lots of movement, and they could not reach it. And if the batter chose to watch the pitch, it would always catch the outside corner of home plate for a called strike three. That night, batter after batter left home plate in complete frustration as they headed back to the dugout.

As good as a pitcher as Tyce was, he brought something far greater to the game as the ultimate team player. I have helped and coached kids through little league into high school years, and I have never witnessed a player like Tyce who not only encouraged teammates but also played catch with those of much less ability. Despite his pitching a no-hitter and getting the walk-off hit to win the game, it never went to his head. This quality of always being there for a teammate made me the proudest. Every time when I was around him, we talked baseball, and I relived so many memories of watching Yogi Berra, Roger Maris, Whitey Ford, Mickey Mantle, Bobby Richardson, along with Elston Howard of the New York Yankees. Tyce studied the game and knew most of the players from all the Major League teams. I am truly blessed to have a grandson with whom I can share such passion of baseball.

He joined FFA as a sophomore and competes on the Chapter Conducting team. Now, as junior in high school, I see a young man all grown up. It is a joy to work with him on the farm in the summers. He is a really well-behaved kid who will achieve all of his goals in life. The word that describes his trait is *trustworthy*.

It has been an awesome experience working with and donating my time to the Oklahoma Food Bank. But the one thing that made it even more special was the time Aidan and Brynna worked alongside me in the Eastern Oklahoma Food Bank in Tulsa. Recently, Justin joined me working at the Laverne Food Pantry, and I cannot wait to work alongside Tyce and Kade at a food pantry in the near future. It has been a joy to serve others with the help of my grandchildren. The verse found in Proverbs 17:6 says it all: "Children's children are the crown of old men; and the glory of children are their fathers." My crown is full!

CHAPTER 4

Pumpkin

O ften times, pumpkins are used at the center of colorful decorations. The round shape and liveliness of their orange color brightens every place that pumpkins are used to decorate. They radiate cheerfulness. Looking down at your sweet, round little face with your huge smile, you had already stolen my heart as a tiny baby. This is why you were nicknamed "Pumpkin." You were that little bundle of joy sent from heaven above for two young parents to enjoy and love.

That early morning, toward the end of your earthly journey, our souls became bonded forever as we stood watching the sun's rays peak over the eastern horizon. Our hands were clasped tightly together and lifted high in praise to our Father, our Lord and Savior. I keep the picture of that day close to my heart. Your gallant fight and determination in battling your own cancer gave me even more strength in fighting my cancer step by step, side by side, every single day. It was my desire to hold you in my arms again, just as I did when you were my little baby. You would fall asleep and feel secure. Even though miles apart, we shared scriptures nightly for that much-needed comfort and security, again.

Your artwork and courage continue to inspire and touch me daily. On that very same hill where we watched the sun rise is a wooden cedar cross, along with a bench that bears your name. It's home, the place your ashes have come to rest. I will always remember the night before you knocked on heaven's door. During that last conversation, you were concerned about my neighbor who had needed help earlier that day. You asked how it went, and I was able to tell you that everything went well and we finished the job for him. Our last words spoken to each other that night were "I love you, good night." I wrote this poem for you, Cherinda, my precious daughter.

Little Pumpkin

This is my story from a father's eyes,
in that day when two souls became one.
Joined hands raised at sunrise,
praising our Savior, Jesus the Son.
Our journey had already started,
with a promise I would stand by you forever.
Let it be me, when the hurdles get too high,
waves too rough, standing together.

This is not a tale of disappointment, empty walls, bad reports,
but of strength and hope.
I am the one left to share that anointed place,
that cross on the hill's slope.
It became evident early on, you had a spirit of courage,
another word, brave.
Many days and nights were devoted,

24

of sharing scriptures that you so craved.
Because in these divine moments we spent together,
I started a game,
Challenging you to come up with Bible characters
most like you to name.

In this Good Book,
many characters and stories exist in the new and old.
There was a trait you possessed
that matched some of these that began to unfold.
Your first guess, Sampson,
strongest, toughest of all time throughout the land.
Mystery hidden in his curly locks,
now blinded, pillars crumbled by his hand.
Might be Jonah, she quizzed me,
but cast and thrown overboard out to sea.
Only to be swallowed by a big fish,
in the belly days and nights times three.
Could it be Paul,
a great writer of several books in the Bible? she thought.
But then she remembered once known as Saul,
Christians who he sought.
I know, it's Moses,
for God gave him the Ten Commandments still used today.
He also parted the Red Sea,
to let the Israelites escape the enemy to get away.
King David, the little shepherd boy,
armed with only a sling and five stones,
Slew Goliath, the giant who stood six cubits,
with a blow to the skull bone.
It's got to be Peter, spokesman for the twelve disciples,
Jesus's right-hand man.

Fisherman who walked on water, denied Jesus,
great preacher in the land.

From a ram's horn you showed me the shofar,
which makes a trumpet sound.
Now knocking on its doors, ushered by 10,000 angels,
you were heaven bound.
Remember on Thanksgiving Day,
Papa's Angels, your fingerprints helped form,
In helping me to find my divine purpose,
to rise above that threatening storm.
You were a rock that spurred me,
to awesome heights in the spiritual realm.
Where things unseen trump things seen,
miracles happen, Jesus at the helm.
Known as Aunt Sissy to a niece,
and four little nephews that you left behind.
Rest assured, they inherited your kindness and compassion,
it's so hard to find.
A gifted artist who used her soul to draw or paint,
where everything just flowed.
Didn't matter if birds, nature, abstract,
the lines and objects danced and glowed.
Your talents included that gentle spirit
that awaited when meeting a friend.
Pure heart, compassion unmatched,
arms extended with a smile and a grin.

Back to our game, you possessed courage,
equal to these four Hebrew men,
Shadrach, Meshach, Abednego in the fiery furnace,
and Daniel in the lion's den.

26

Your footprints will never fade away,
your legacy of life will continue to grow.
Your spirit hovers over us at sunrise,
blue birds on the cross, sparkles in the snow.
A quiet place high up on the hill,
bench with the cross, a time to reflect and pray.
Giving thanks for such a precious gift,
awaiting for our reunion on that day.

In loving memory to Cherinda
—Dad

IT IS WELL WITH MY SOUL

CHAPTER 5

It Is Well with My Soul

I n late May 2011, I was sitting all alone in my doctor's office anxiously waiting for the appointment with my PA, Steve Madrid. He listened intently to me as I told him of the recent health concern I had. It had occurred a week earlier in Waxahachie, Texas, while visiting my daughter, Kareece, and her husband, Derek, and sons, Tyce and Kade. Steve and I chatted for a few more minutes as he ordered a blood test and a CT scan for the next day at the Harper County Community Hospital in Buffalo, Oklahoma.

The next day while I was lying on the table waiting to enter the scan chamber, I saw a sign appear right above me as though it was suspended in air. It was about six inches high and twenty-four inches in length. It had the words *IT IS WELL WITH MY SOUL* written on it in bold letters. It looked just like the road signs that appear along the highways in Northwest Oklahoma that identify our towns, like Slapout, Gate, Laverne, Buffalo, and Fort Supply. Moments later, I entered the CT machine for the procedure. It was a short scan, and soon I was reeled back out. I immediately glanced up to read the sign again, but it had disappeared.

The following day, the test results revealed I had renal cell kidney cancer. This set in motion a journey that involved many doctor appointments, grim reports, and surgeries. But, through that sign, God had revealed to me that despite all that was about to happen, everything would be well with my soul.

Fast forward to August 6, 2017, at the Assembly of God Church in Mooreland, Oklahoma. Pastor Phillip Ludwyck and his wife, Jama, had invited my niece Cynthia McGuire Murphy and her husband, Marc, along with two of their friends from Ireland, Jacqui Orr and Breda Judge, to help lead the worship service. Cynthia and Marc are both pastors and missionaries who were living in Ireland at the time. The praise and worship that kicked off this service ushered in the Holy Spirit. Marc preached an inspirational sermon titled "Slaying Giants." He reminded us that the enemy will try to steal God's blessings from us. Marc encouraged us to be bold and to always stand up and be ready to fight, because we can defeat the enemy.

The enemy is always lurking and ready to pounce on any weakness at any moment. Satan is so evil. It is so important in our Christian walk that we are bold in our actions and always ready to fight back. There are a host of ungodly things out in this world that will distract us if we turn our eyes away from Jesus. The only way to become immune to the devil's wicked ways and to defeat him is through the gospel of Jesus Christ. Studying and reading scriptures in the Bible on a daily basis helps form that protection we need to be kept safe from Satan's evil intent. Our daily prayer life and devotion must always remain strong in order to keep Satan stomped and defeated in our lives.

At the close of the service, Cynthia and Jacqui sang the song "It Is Well with My Soul." The harmony of their voices blended with the music and created an anointed sound that only this duo could make. I closed my eyes as my mind drifted back to that day in May 2011, when I saw the sign in that tiny room in the Harper County Community Hospital. My heavenly Father had spoken that promise to me. Now, six years later, He reminded me of it yet again: it is well with my soul. Before they sang the final song, Cynthia mentioned during practice the night before that God had revealed to them that someone the next day would be blessed when they heard the song. After the service, I got to share with them how much this song meant to me and the vision I had seen. Thank you so much, Cynthia and Jacqui, for obeying the Holy Spirit in choosing that song that allowed me to relive the vision again. I pray blessings upon that awesome Irish team. "And it shall come to pass in the last days, saith God, I will pour out of my Spirit upon all flesh: and your sons and your daughters shall prophesy, and your young men shall see visions, and your old men shall dream dreams" (Acts 2:17). This verse reminds us that we will never stand alone.

The hymn "It Is Well with My Soul" was written in 1873 by Horatio Spafford. He wrote this song after a tragedy at sea occurred on November 22, 1873, when the ocean liner his wife and four daughters were traveling on was hit by a British vessel and sank within minutes. His wife was rescued, but his four young daughters drowned in the Atlantic Ocean. He was detained by business in Chicago at the time and received the news by cable nine days after the accident. His wife sent the message, "Saved alone. What shall I do?" Horatio departed at once to join to wife. During the sea crossing, the captain of the ship showed him the exact area where the shipwreck had occurred and his daughters had perished. He returned to his cabin and wrote these words of comfort and hope:

When peace like a river attendeth my way,
When sorrows like sea billows roll;
Whatever my lot, Thou has taught me to say,
It is well, it is well with my soul.

Refrain:
It is well with my soul,
It is well, it is well with my soul.

Though Satan should buffet, though trials should come,
Let this blest assurance control,
That Christ has regarded my helpless estate,
And hath shed his own blood for my soul.

My sin, oh, the bliss of this glorious thought!
My sin, not in part but the whole,
Is nailed to the cross, and I bear it no more,
Praise the Lord, praise the Lord, O my soul!

And, Lord, haste the day when my faith shall be sight,
The clouds be rolled back as a scroll;
The trump shall resound, and the Lord shall descend,
Even so, it is well with my soul!

CHAPTER 6

Nuts and Bolts

I nstilled in me is that old farmer mentality to store stuff that, in most cases, is really worn out. It is hard to throw anything away just in case it might come in handy someday. Hidden behind the shop, along a row of trees, all sorts of abandoned equipment rests tangled among the woods. A few of the trees have smaller items leaning up against their trunks. Oftentimes, branches grow through the openings of the discarded junk. I have to be very careful walking through this maze because I just might step on an old rotten wooden pallet, or a partial roll of barbed wire, or a few sheets of rusty barn tin.

Once inside the shop, at the far end of a work bench sits an old coffee can filled to the brim with different sizes of old nails, and over somewhere in the shop corner sits a five-gallon bucket filled with rusty old nuts, washers, and bolts used to secure sweep blades, chisel points, plows, or perhaps the planter from years before. Over many years, a variety of different sizes and lengths of nuts and bolts have accumulated. After twenty or thirty years, there's the off chance they might finally come in handy for a quick fix of broken pieces of machinery or equipment to help me avoid a trip to town for repairs. Numerous times, way too many to count, I have scraped the skin off my knuckles trying to pry and twist these rusty worn-out nuts from the bolts. Nowadays, all garages and shop buildings have small storage bins or organizers to separate each size of the nuts and bolts. Those bins are located somewhere on a work bench or on shelves built onto the wall. Just imagine our lives today without these nuts and bolts; we simply could not exist in this world as we know it.

For example, our cars and trucks are put together with all sizes and types of nuts and bolts. Tiny ones are used to fasten the battery cables to the battery posts; they must be secured tightly and not become corroded in order to get that juice to the ignition when starting the vehicle. Next, the starter is held in place by longer bolts that are next to the flywheel; if the bolts become loose, our car or truck will not start. The starter is crucial. What about the lug nuts attached to the stud bolts on the wheel? They must be snugged tightly so that they don't become loose or fall off. Our rims with the tires securely fastened are a must in our travels. Likewise, the tractors and implements we use to put up our hay crops and cultivate and harvest our fields depend on numerous nuts and bolts in order to operate and work properly. By now you get the picture—it takes many nuts and bolts all working together to provide our transportation. It's vital to take our kids to school, to attend school sporting events, to go shopping, to go to the movies, or to visit our favorite coffee shops and malls. But most important of all, they enable us to attend our church activities.

To all my friends and relatives who served in the Vietnam War, it's time to mention the story of a very famous nut that got its name during this era. It was first called, and soon after became known as, the Jesus Nut. Over seven thousand Hueys, the UH-1 Iroquois helicopters, flew during this war. The Jesus

Nut was a fist-sized main rotor retaining nut which held the main rotor to the mast of each Huey. If for some reason it would loosen and fail, it would certainly have catastrophic results. As for how the nut got its name, the story goes that a soldier asked an aircraft mechanic, "What would happen if it were to come off?" The mechanic's answer was simple and to the point. He stated, "Start praying to Jesus." Without this nut, the helicopter would become disabled, resulting in a very quick plummet and crash to the ground below. The word "Jesus Nut" got around rather quickly to all the troops and became widely known.

Just as many of these soldiers' lives depended on this famous nut, our spiritual lives also depend on spiritual nuts and bolts. They are essential to fasten and hold together our Christian values as we live in today's world while walking with our heavenly Father upon this earth. While serving our Master, the first thing we find out is that all our gossip, pride, and anger cannot be hidden at the bottom of that old bucket anymore. This pile of junk, which once cluttered our lives, must now be thrown away in order to serve Him. I must now mention that, first and foremost, I believe in the Trinity; I believe that God as the Father is the first person, followed by the second person, the Son, Jesus Christ, and the third person, the Holy Spirit. As we have discovered the importance of nuts and bolts in the physical world, God has shown me that the spiritual nuts and bolts are equally vital in the spiritual realm as well.

God has provided blueprints, very similar to the diagrams found in our many parts manuals that help to maintain our machinery. Let's look in the toolbox God has provided. As we peek inside, we see seven powerful words that are given to help us model the way to live our lives. The first word we find written is *Father*. In the book of Matthew 6:9-13 (NKJV), we find the Lord's prayer:

Our Father in heaven, hallowed be Your name. Your kingdom come. Your will be done on earth as it is in heaven. Give us this day our daily bread. And forgive us our debts, as we forgive our debtors. And do not lead us into temptation, but deliver us from the evil one. For Yours is the kingdom and the power and the glory forever. Amen.

Each day as I walk on this hallowed ground, I continually seek His guidance in all things. Another scripture found in the book of James 1:17 (NKJV) states, "Every good gift and every perfect gift is from above, and comes down from the Father of lights, with whom there is no variation or shadow of turning." These two passages help to keep me grounded as I go about my daily chores on the farm. No matter what task awaits me, my heavenly Father is with me.

The second written word in my tool box is *faith*. We find in Romans 12:3 that God has given "to every man the measure of faith." It's now up to me to act upon and believe God's Word. Romans 10:17 states, "So then faith cometh by hearing, and hearing by the Word of God." Likewise, in Hebrews 11:6 (NASB), we learn: "And without faith it is impossible to please Him, for he who comes to God must believe that He is and that He is a rewarder of those who seek Him." We also find in 2 Timothy 4:7 (NIV): "I have fought the good fight, I have finished the race, I have kept the faith." These scriptures will boost and develop that level of trust and confidence needed to grow by hearing His Word. At some point in our lives, all of us will face the agony of defeat along with that sweet taste of victory. It is how we handle these ups and downs as Christians in His army of overcomers that is so important.

The third word is *forgiveness*. We have a huge range of emotions stored within us. Our changes in attitude can go full circle in a very short period of time: from sad to glad and from joy to anger. My entire life has centered around sports, from participating in them to supporting my children and now my grandchildren. As a parent and as a fan, I have heard boos directed toward the officials along with lots of complaints made against the coaches. I think we all can plead guilty to doing this at some point in our lives! We must remember to take control of our actions and take responsibility for our behavior at all times.

As a farmer, I have seen disputes over fence boundaries and arguments over business dealings. It is important to listen to our inner spirit and be slow to anger. Sometimes we need to walk away instead of quarrel. There will be times when we need to ask for forgiveness. A good scripture is found in Ephesians 4:31–32 (NIV): "Get rid of all bitterness, rage and anger, brawling and slander, along with every form of malice. Be kind and compassionate to one another, forgiving each other, just as in Christ God forgave you." Remember that in most situations that confront us and then get totally out of control, it is our tongues that spit out hurtful words, which are never forgotten.

The fourth word is *foundation*. We must build a strong spiritual foundation that will withstand all negative forces that try to cause cracks to form and weaken that rock upon which we stand. Time spent in prayer and reading the Word of God will help strengthen that foundation to endure the forces of deceit, conflict, wickedness, and corruption that pound against it. Oftentimes in my life as a farmer, additional stress is caused by hail, drought, and commodity price drops in both wheat and cattle. Even the insects and other pests can take a heavy toll. It's during these rough patches that we find strength and solace in the book Isaiah 28:16 (NASB): "Therefore thus says the Lord God, 'Behold, I am laying in Zion a stone, a tested stone, a costly cornerstone for the foundation, firmly placed. He who believes in it will not be disturbed.'"

The fifth word is *fellowship*. It is so important to find a church that will allow you to flourish and grow spiritually in Christ. Finding that church family to share time with is critical. The church family will provide that solid rock for when the road becomes a bit weary. In times of sickness or when a family member passes away, the church family will surround you and help share your burdens and grief. We find in Matthew 18:20: "For where two or three are gathered together in my name, there am I in the midst of them." Once sitting inside the sanctuary listening to God's spoken words and His praise and worship songs, all the negative forces on the outside will fade and melt away.

The sixth word found is *fervent* in *prayer*. The gift that we all receive as born-again Christians is our very own direct, open, personal prayer line to God. It is so important to let Him know what's really on our hearts and to tell Him all our prayer requests—anytime and anywhere. Our prayer language can vary from crying out to Him to praising Him and giving thanks to Him. It doesn't matter if it is vocal or a whispering silent prayer; our God will hear. We find in Jeremiah 29:12 (NASB): "Then you will call upon Me and come and pray to Me, and I will listen to you." Also, in 1 Thessalonians 5:17 we are told to "pray without ceasing." Likewise, Philippians 4:6 (NIV) tells us, "Do not be anxious about anything, but in every situation, by prayer and petition, with thanksgiving, present your requests to God."

The final and seventh word is *fruit*. We find in Matthew 12:33 (NKJV): "Either make the tree good and its fruit good, or else make the tree bad and its fruit bad; for a tree is known by its fruit." As a wheat farmer, it is important to plant clean seed each year. One seed will produce several tillers, and on the end of each tiller, a seed head will flourish and produce wheat for harvest. Each seed may produce twenty-fold, forty-fold, or sixty-fold. Wheat farmers check on their fields regularly after the wheat starts to joint and grow in the late spring. After the wheat starts to head out and the seeds start to grow, it takes about six weeks for it to ripen and be ready to harvest. Many times, as you drive by a field, you might see a farmer standing in his field checking on the progress of his crop.

We as Christians must strive to be like the fruit found in Galatians 5:22–23 (NKJV): "But the fruit of the Spirit is love, joy, peace, longsuffering, kindness, goodness, faithfulness, gentleness, self-control. Against such there is no law." This is the fruit I seek each day. Ask yourself today:

Have I helped my neighbor who is sick or in need?

Have I assisted that stranded motorist with a flat?

Have I driven a sick friend to the doctor?

Have I reached out to the family who lost their loved one?

Have I fed or clothed someone who was hungry or cold?

Remember these seven bold words found in the spiritual nuts and bolts manual. When we walk each step, the soles of our shoes will touch down on that strong foundation. It was formed for us to be shielded and protected from the storms that will come our way. The words found in the scriptures help us recognize our mistakes and wrongdoings. When we seek out our Father above and ask Him for forgiveness from our transgressions, we will be forgiven. As Christians, it's awesome to share in fellowship with other believers to witness His power as we pray together in fervent prayer. I would like to encourage you to always produce the best fruit possible in your daily life. Could you imagine the harvest that will come from these tiny spiritual seeds?

Keep up the good faith in living this glorious life serving in His kingdom on this earth.

CHAPTER 7

Bois-D'arc

The Bois-D'arc tree, also known as Osage orange, grows in the high plains of the Oklahoma Panhandle. Its wood is extremely hard and durable. Hidden inside the rough outer edge is a beautiful, yellow-orange color wood.

For many years, the Native American Indians that roamed and settled in this area made their hunting bows from this tough wood. Later, when the settlers homesteaded here during the land runs, they built fences to form the boundaries of their new property. Oftentimes, Bois-D'arc wood was cut and used for both line and corner posts for their fences. These well-cured wooden fenceposts could last a hundred years. Hand dug, planted, and tamped into the ground, these posts were not pretty, but rather twisted and crooked. They served their purpose well, though, in providing solid anchors to stretch new barbed wire across.

Those old posts were slammed by tumbleweeds and hammered by the forces of the wind's fury. Rain and hail constantly pounded the fences again and again. Yet, that old Bois-D'arc corner post did not ever shake. It always stood firm and withstood the test of time. A verse found in Luke 6:48 (ESV) reminds me that "he is like a man building a house, who dug deep and laid the foundation on the rock. And when a flood arose, the stream broke against that house and could not shake it, because it had been well built."

The Bois-D'arc posts are so solid and dense that they do not rot underneath the ground. These hedge posts were very popular in the early 1900s and are still in great demand today. The only drawback to using these posts is that it is nearly impossible to staple the wire to them because of their density. It is much easier to use wire to wrap each strand of barbed wire to each post.

That old era of building fences with Bois-D'arc posts has been updated, using new materials. Now cedar or creosote posts are very practical to use. Combining coal tar with heat under a high-oven process, the creosote oil penetrates throughout the wood and protects it against wood rot and insect damage. Both cedar and creosote posts are softer than Bois-D'arc and easier to hammer staples into. In our area, creosote posts are more popular. Lately, four- to six-inch heavy-walled pipes set in concrete are being used for corner posts instead of wood. The fences built today are much sturdier than those built in the beginning of our statehood. Back in the early 1900s, wooden posts were set about eighteen feet apart, but now we set posts ten feet apart. Today's fences feature metal t-posts with angled studs to make it easier to secure the wire to the fence with clips. Back in the early days, most fences only had three strands of barbed wire or four at the most. Now, we use five to seven strands of wire. But, no matter what the future of fence building has to offer, there will always be a place for the Bois-D'arc posts.

Each winter while feeding cows in a certain pasture, I occasionally stop to admire that old Bois-D'arc post that still stands tall and rock solid. It has withstood many decades and every-thing Mother Nature has dished out. That old post reminds me just how important it is in our Christian walk to build a strong foundation just like those old corner posts of long ago. What an awesome God we serve, who gives us the words written in the scriptures that help us to design and build our foundation. It will never crumble but will always stand the test of time.

CHAPTER 8

How Full Is Your Barn?

We find in Deuteronomy 28:8 (NASB): "The Lord will command the blessing upon you in your barns and in all that you put your hand to, and He will bless you in the land which the Lord your God gives you." Driving throughout the countryside with this scripture etched in my mind, I always take notice how my neighbors store their hay crops. I have seen small, square bales stuffed into small sheds, in lean-tos attached to sheds, and even in old school houses. Basically, you will likely see hay bales stacked in anything that has a roof to help keep the hay dry.

My life has always been centered around hay fields, whether it was alfalfa, grass, sorghum-sudan, or millet. In other words, just about anything a cow will eat, we have grown it and wrapped it up into small square or big round bales. After nearly sixty years working in the hay field, I have a few memories that I will never forget. Once, my friend and classmate fell through a loose board in the hay loft of the barn. He landed about ten feet below and cracked his tailbone. As I recall, we quit work for the rest of the day. The only other serious injury occurred when my cousin Alan got thrown from the back of the hay truck and broke his arm.

Everyone who has ever bucked square bales has endured painful blisters either on their fingers or more likely on the palms of their hands just below where the fingers attach. It usually takes several days and lots of white tape before the hands start to toughen up and calluses form to help prevent more blisters from forming during the rest of the summer. This scene is repeated each year after the first cutting. To all of you out there who have ever hauled and stacked bales, you know exactly what I'm talking about.

The longest day ever of hauling hay occurred during the end of my junior year in high school. The night before was our junior-senior prom. After it was over, we all moved to the drive-in theater for the rest of the night. I remember making it back home in time to crawl into bed around 5:00 a.m. An hour later, my dad walked in and turned on the light to let me know breakfast was ready. Since he had baled hay all night, there were bales that needed to be hauled as soon as we had eaten. I remember exactly how many bales I loaded by myself on the back of the truck that day—1,510. With my cousin Reta Sue driving, I loaded six loads at 151 bales per load before we stopped for lunch. That afternoon, we hauled four more loads, bringing the total to 1,510 bales. Reta's husband, the late Jerry Hoover, helped my uncle Calvin unload and stack the hay into the huge hayshed. By the end of the day, my hands were raw with blisters. Jerry removed his gloves, and his blisters went all the way across both hands. It looked as if he had blisters on top of his blisters.

My dad, Delvin, and Uncle Calvin always wore long-sleeved shirts to protect their arms from the alfalfa stems and the hot sun. I, being in high school, chose to wear short-sleeve t-shirts.

I suppose it was to show off my deeply tanned guns to the girls, even though I was covered with countless scratches from the hay and was sunburnt from the scorching summer sun.

Once, we lost a load of hay turning into the gate at my dad's hayshed less than thirty yards from our destination. It was lots of work and time spent driving those same thirty yards back and forth, reloading the truck just to unload and stack the bales again. Both my dad and uncle had haysheds that stood probably eighteen feet tall at the peak and measured thirty-four feet wide by fifty-six feet long. Each shed would hold approximately 6,210 + 1 bales. One time, after we completely filled my dad's hayshed, I was determined to fit just one more bale inside: I wedged it into the very top of the rafters. That bale really stood the test of time. It remained there for over forty years, long after the hay shed stood empty. A couple years ago, a high wind brought the structure down. My grandson Justin thought we should save that antique alfalfa bale covered with years of dust and do something special with it. So, we fed it to the goats.

The biggest lesson I received in hay hauling came from my uncle Calvin. It was getting close to the end of the era where we stacked each bale by hand. That day, it was just my uncle and me putting hay into the hayloft of his barn. As I recall, we had three truckloads to stack on that very hot, steamy day. He drove the truck while I loaded the first load before we headed back to the barn. I normally pitched the hay into the loft. This was very difficult to do from the bottom three tiers on the truck. You had to stair step up and then lift each bale up about four feet to the loft floor opening. Normally, we would have two on the truck and two stacking inside the loft. But, this day was much more challenging because it was just the two of us. Nearly getting done with the first load, I casually mentioned to Calvin that he really had it made because he was in the shade and I was in the sweltering heat. He just looked at me and kind of nodded his head. We headed back to the field, and I loaded again as he drove. When we got back to the barn, he quickly hopped out of the truck and got on top of the load, leaving me to head up to the hayloft. The barn had a tin roof, and the heat inside that loft, I swear, must have been 125 degrees without any air circulation. It was absolutely suffocating, and beads of sweat poured from my head. After getting this load into the loft, we headed back to the field, where I loaded hay as Calvin drove. We arrived back to the barn, where my uncle resumed his position in the loft as I pitched the bales up to him. I realized that day that he had the harder job inside that oven than I had on the back of the truck. Without uttering a word, he showed me that his job was much tougher and hotter than mine, and he did it without a single complaint. I will always treasure that memory.

For the majority of three decades, my dad, Delvin, Uncle Calvin, cousin Alan, and I were the main hay crew. We stacked thousands of square bales. Thinking back to those days, we all were in great shape. Due to the age of our fathers and the new technology available, we decided to hire a neighbor with a stack machine to take over for the next several years. Later on, we began using mostly round bales. It took a lot of convincing for my dad to see that this would be much easier and better for both of us when feeding cattle in the winters.

Now that we have looked at our physical hay crop stored in our sheds and barns, I pray that your spiritual storehouse is as full as our barn. We find in Malachi 3:10 (NIV): "'Bring the whole tithe into the storehouse, that there may be food in my house. Test me in this,' says the Lord Almighty, 'and see if I will not throw open the floodgates of heaven and pour out so much blessing that there will not be room enough to store it.'"

CHAPTER 9

Mending Fences

Without a doubt, the hardest chore for me on the ranch is repairing broken wires on an old fence. Many times, it starts with two old bulls snorting and pawing at the dirt on opposite sides of the fence. They try to get at each other and end up fighting. It never ceases to amaze me just how much fence two tons of beast can tear up. When the dust settles in the aftermath of their mayhem, wooden posts are broken off and lay splintered on the ground. The barbed wire is pulled apart and strands lay broken and tangled everywhere. The six-foot steel t-posts are bent over, and the bulls are nowhere in sight. Now, my work begins. I use post-hole diggers to dig new holes to plant new posts. Broken wires are sifted through and spliced back together before I can stretch them as tight as before. Next, I have to drive staples into the new wood posts with a hammer to secure the wire. Finally, the t-posts are pulled or pushed back into line and the wire clips attached to each post.

By now, you get the picture, only this scene is played out repeatedly over the years. It might be 100 degrees in the heat of summer or 20 degrees in the freezing cold of winter, but no matter what the temperature is outside, the job must be done. Unfortunately, just like our fences on the ranch that are broken and in need of repair from time to time, sometimes our spiritual fences need to be mended too. Our human nature and the emotions in us can cause many problems. It starts out when we are little children, fighting over the same toy. Years later, as mature adults, we still fight. Sometimes with actions, but mostly by speaking harmful words. These spiteful words are like daggers that pierce our souls. As a result, hurt feelings are hard to overcome and, in many cases, never forgotten.

There are a host of things that damage our spiritual fences and can cause them to break. These breaks happen when our trust in someone becomes frayed, perhaps by jealousy or broken promises. Many times, the emotions of joy and happiness that enrich our souls are stolen and taken away from us. When pride takes control and rules, it becomes nearly impossible to be rational and willing to admit our wrongdoing. This makes it that much tougher to mend our fences and forgive. In this life, we often face many broken relationships.

Shortly after being diagnosed with cancer, God revealed to me that I needed to make a list of all the names of those I had gossiped about, bullied, and made fun of. My list of names grew as I recalled every hurt that I had caused others from high school to the present time. Now, with the completed list of names, I laid it before my Lord and Savior. I asked for His forgiveness for every hurtful word and deed that I had committed. When I was finished, the Lord told me, "You forgot one."

This was harder than any fence repair I had ever done on the ranch. Going directly to another person and to ask for forgiveness is very hard to do. In this case, he was a neighbor I had known my entire life. It became very easy to just ignore the whole situation, but in reality, I was not man enough to face him. I rationalized in my mind that it was not the proper time to go and that I could put it off until sometime in the distant future. Every night, I wrestled with God about this, but God would win. (When you wrestle with God, you will always lose.) The rest of the story is that our paths crossed shortly after this, and I asked my good friend and neighbor for forgiveness. And he forgave me.

We find scripture in our spiritual fence toolbox that equips us to repair and mend these relationships. The first scripture is found in James 1:19: "Wherefore, my beloved brethren, let every man be swift to hear, slow to speak, slow to wrath." Also, in Galatians 5:22–23, it is written: "But the fruit of the Spirit is love, joy, peace, longsuffering, gentleness, goodness, faith, meekness, temperance: against such there is no law." My prayer today is that all of our fences, both spiritual and physical, will be completely mended and restored as we walk this journey on our Father's path. Amen.

CHAPTER 10

Signs and Wonders

Growing up as a small child, I was always attracted to dirt. My mother told me that this fascination began as a toddler, when I would grab dirt with my hands and bring it to my mouth. When I was a little older, many afternoons were spent watering Grandmother Beryl's fruit trees. I carefully constructed channels and dams around each tree, and once they were connected, I turned on the garden hose and filled the reservoirs with water. Soon, it was time to open the floodgates I had made of rocks and sticks to let the water flow from tree to tree.

It was during this time that my first cousin, Reta Sue, recruited me to be the new head chef and cook at her outdoor restaurant. Linda, Reta Sue's little sister, also worked at this restaurant. Since Reta Sue was older than both of us, she was automatically the owner of this operation. Under a shade tree in Uncle Calvin and Aunt Irma's front yard, our enterprise thrived. Reta Sue helped Linda take orders and visited with our many customers. She also checked on me in the kitchen area. I don't recall the entire menu, but what I do remember is our famous chocolate mud pies.

With a few pots and pans, a pile of dirt, and a bucket of water, we blended this mixture into some of the most awesome, mouth-watering pies that we served daily. Our make-believe customers who dined with us were treated to special toppings on their favorite piece of chocolate pie. Sometimes we used small sticks, and at other times, we used an assortment of small rocks to create that yummy taste. But, our most prized dessert, and a delight to all our wonderful customers, was that extra special pie topped with a rich layer of creamy, white sticky puff-ball, with just a touch of brown. To this very day, we have never revealed our unique, secret mix for the grandest of all our pie toppings. Since it has been nearly sixty years, I guess it's time to disclose where we found the secret topping for our wonderful dessert pies that we made under that tall elm tree: *next to our restaurant was Aunt Irma's chicken house.*

Later in life, the experiences as a young boy playing in the dirt would teach me the fascination of God's creation that captures the beauty of our land. The sun, the moon, and the stars surround me each and every day. We find in Genesis 1:1: "In the beginning God created the heavens and the earth." Each day, from sunrise to sunset, God reveals all His majesty and the beauty of His creation. To witness our heavenly Father's creativity, to know that He holds us all in the palm of His hand and that He shows each of us the splendor that exists in the four seasons, is powerful. Our Father reminds us in Genesis 8:22 (NKJV), "While the earth remains, seedtime and harvest, cold and heat, winter and summer, and day and night shall not cease." Also, the scripture found in John 1:3 (NKJV) tells us, "All things were made through Him, and without Him nothing was made that was made." Likewise, Psalm 95:4–5 (NKJV) reads, "In His hand are the deep places of the earth; the heights of the hills are His also. The sea is His, for He made it; and His hands formed the dry land."

As a farmer-rancher, I realize that we will face natural disasters that will plague us from time to time. But, I also know that neither these floods, droughts, nor even tornadoes can permanently take away the beauty of His creation. Tending to my chores on a daily basis, He reminds me of the wonders that capture the vastness of what He has created. Each of the four seasons show me His wonders on the farm. Let's first examine the fall season, when the leaves on the trees begin to change color, from green to a golden color and then to brown, as they dry up and fall gently to the earth's floor. The landscape is rapidly changing from the summer growing season to a season where wildflowers and grass lose their color. The beauty of golden hedge-apples that have fallen from the trees and lay dispersed on a bit of grass will soon serve as a source of food for the deer, squirrels, and other wildlife. These fall days, I hear the sandhill crane and catch a glimpse of their V-shaped formation flying south to their new winter home. I finally have to break out my warm jacket as the north wind ushers in a chill of much cooler air. The days become shorter as the sun shifts farther south in the sky.

Now, the cold fronts usher in much cooler temperatures, setting the winter season in motion. On a calm winter morning, the sun's rays pierce through the bare trees and paint the silhouette of their branches against the dirt canvas. Driving down the road, I startle a covey of quail that takes flight and glides across the fence to the other side to nestle in the weeds and grass out of sight. I look forward to seeing the beautiful sight of deer grazing on lush green wheat, and, of course, I'm always on the lookout for the rack of a monster buck. It is always great to feel the warmth of the sun while standing behind a windbreak protected from the north wind or while driving my pickup, feeling the sun shine through the window.

Oh, what beauty it is to watch the first snowflakes drop gently from the gray overcast sky. Not often, but once in a great while, I get to see the snow stacked high on the tops of the cedar posts that line a fence or the sight of rabbits and their fresh tracks left from a night of dancing in the fallen snow. Winter has its drawbacks. It gets really muddy from the rain or melting snow and sometimes makes extra chores like chopping ice on the cattle water and feeding extra hay for the cows. But, there is nothing more beautiful than watching the stars twinkle and glow up in the sky on a cold winter's night while listening to the howl of a coyote in the distance.

Hurry up, spring! I can't wait for the days to start getting longer again as southerly winds start ushering in warmer temperatures. Soon, the wildflowers start to bloom, and new buds appear on the trees. The songs of the meadowlarks fill the air and signal that spring is here. The sight of a newborn, wobbly-legged calf standing up for the first time next to its mama is very special. I really enjoy the sound of the deep rumbles of thunder as lightning flashes across the sky and the smell of that sweet aroma of sagebrush in the clean, fresh air after a spring shower. It is awesome to hear the calls of the sandhill cranes as they return to the northern regions for their summer home. My favorite time of spring is always Easter Sunday, when we celebrate that our Lord and Savior has risen. He is *alive!*

Very soon, the summer season will be here. The temperatures rise, and the heat starts to build, with much longer days ushering in the busiest time of my year. Hay is cut and baled for next winter's supply. The wheat crops are harvested, and fields are plowed and prepped for planting in the fall. The orchestra sound created by frogs as they sing after a heavy rain makes for some of the best music I have ever heard. Some of the most beautiful portraits ever created are the multicolored rainbows that grace our skies after a rain shower. To see the green grass dotted with the vibrant colors of wildflowers that cover my pastures is a sight that I cherish. Spread throughout the fields, herds of cows grazing with their young calves nearby never fail to bring me joy. Many times, I park my truck just to watch a mother turkey hen and her little chicks scratch for bugs and tiny grasshoppers in the grass. She does an amazing job watching this year's hatchlings as they scurry everywhere.

During my many years on this small spread, God speaks to me daily through all of these signs and wonders and through His Word found in Romans 1:20 (NASB): "For since the creation of the world, His invisible attributes, His eternal power and divine nature, have been clearly seen, being understood through what has been made, so that they are without excuse." Another favorite scripture, Genesis 1:24 (NKJV), reveals more about God's creation. "Then God said, 'Let the earth bring forth the living creature according to its kind: cattle and creeping thing and beast of the earth, each according to its kind; and it was so.'" I have been blessed many times over in observing the amazing handiwork that my Lord and Savior has provided me over the decades of tending to my chores.

CHAPTER 11

Lamb's Book of Life

It was in the spring of 2012, when I had a vision that to this day still remains etched in my memory. Let me share with you one of the most amazing things that I have ever witnessed. Standing before me was a stairway leading to an entrance to a courtyard in heaven. I saw a flight of stairs fourteen feet wide and twelve steps high that had been carved out of wood. This was not just any ordinary wood; nothing on this earth even compares. The wood grain appeared three-dimensional, raising above the wood itself. The glossy finish glowed and illuminated the rail and stairs. Reaching out and touching this piece of wooden stairway, I was totally amazed to feel that it was silky smooth. After climbing up one flight of stairs to a landing deck, I turned west to climb another set of these beautifully carved stairs.

When I reached the top, I stepped into an open-air courtyard that was sixty feet wide by eighty feet long. The low walls that enclosed this special place were made of carved white stone. Mounted onto these stone walls were wooden benches made out of the same three-dimensional, glossy wood as the staircases.

On the southwest corner stood a huge tree with large, dark grain branches with soft, velvet green-colored leaves which provided shade over the entire courtyard. I sat on a bench midway down the courtyard on the right side. Other people sat on benches that were scattered and dispersed along all four sides of the courtyard.

I waited patiently as names were being called. I got up occasionally to explore more of the amazing surroundings. Looking down on the street below, I saw many people strolling about. Everything was so pristine—no dust, no litter, no wind. A sweet fragrance filled the air. I saw a magnificent, white stone building with pillars as corners. Finally, my name was called. I walked to the center of the courtyard to view my name written in this large book setting on a flat slab of white stone. The pages appeared to be made out of a type of thin, transparent material. Glancing down at the pages opened wide, there it appeared: my name written in bold print. It read: **KARL JETT**

In Revelation 21:27, there is a book that exists in the heavenly realm that belongs to Jesus Christ, and it is called the Lamb's Book of Life. We find in Revelation 3:5: "He that overcometh, the same shall be clothed in white raiment; and I will not blot out his name out of the book of life, but I will confess his name before my Father, and before his angels."

CHAPTER 12

Me and My Sorting Stick

Everyone that owns cattle has a sorting stick of some type. They come in many shapes and styles. I have seen stock canes, fiberglass poles, plastic paddles, carved tree branches, and on occasion, even a broken shovel handle being used. No matter what we use, though, it is usually stored behind our pickup seat. I have witnessed just about everything when sorting these four-legged beasts over the years. Shouting, hollering, and choice words echo through the air, as if the cattle understand what is being said. I picked up many colorful words and lingo from the sale barns at a very young age when I went with my dad. His favorite slang was to holler, "You ole rip!" It was used for all cattle: steers, heifers, bulls, and cows. These are the same three words that I yell at my cattle to this day while waving my fiberglass pole high in the air.

Anyone who walks into an alleyway or sorting pen is subject to an injury at some point. Getting hit in the head by the backside of the steel gate has been the source of many stitches on the forehead and the cause of a concussion or two. It is common for fingers and hands to get crushed in a working chute. I have known many cowboys who were injured from getting bucked off a horse. Four wheelers are just as dangerous. Many riders over the years have broken backs, ribs, and legs. Some have even gotten a few teeth knocked out by hitting a cow path at high speeds while chasing a stray out in the pasture. Cowboys on horseback have even lost a thumb or a finger when it got caught in the rope as they looped the dally to the saddle horn. Many times, I've been standing in the middle of the pen with just my sorting stick between me and a seven hundred pound wild-eyed, bellowing, dirt-pawing animal charging directly toward me. I have just a split second to decide whether to run or stand my ground.

I would like to share a few of my favorite stories from the past that still make me chuckle to this day. Once, a young bull developed a very bad attitude. We had him shut up in the corral alongside some cows. After selling these cows, he remained behind. Up until this point, he had not been any trouble, but that soon changed. One morning, as I carried an alfalfa bale of hay to the feeder in the middle of the pen, his bad attitude started suddenly. Just as I neared the feeder, out of the corner of my eye, I saw him start pawing the dirt and throwing his head up. He charged rapidly toward me. I jumped to the opposite side of the feeder but soon realized that he wasn't stopping his charge. He was rounding the feeder and was almost upon me. I didn't have time to make a break for the fence, so I attempted to outrun him around the feeder. After three laps, I realized that he was gaining ground on me. I had nowhere else to go, so I had to make a run for it. The nearest fence was probably less than twenty-five feet away, but it seemed like 100 yards. Running as fast as I could, I got close enough to leap the last few feet to clear the five-foot panel. As my momentum carried me over it, the bull headbutted my feet as he crashed into the fence. The force of the impact bent the panel between the two wooden posts. Needless to say, the bull went to the sale barn the next week.

The funniest thing I recall was the time my dad and I went with the pickup and trailer to bring in a sick cow. She was very old and sick, and we needed to doctor her back at the house. Since she was standing out in the pasture all alone as we approached her, my dad decided that he would get out of the pickup and slip the loop of the lariat around her neck. All went just fine until the rope clenched tightly around her neck. The moment she felt the pressure, she lurched forward and took off at a dead run. My dad couldn't keep up. He lost his footing and fell to the ground, but he did not let go of the rope. He held on to it with both hands as he was being dragged through the sagebrush into a draw. I tried to ease my way to head her off as she came up on the other side with my dad still in tow. I could see his head bob up occasionally as they plowed through the pasture. The cow changed directions a few times before I finally managed to pull up even with her. I grabbed the rope and shifted the pickup into neutral as I got out to tie it around the back of the trailer. We soon got her loaded. I glanced over at my dad as he just sat there silently. His face was covered in scratches, both arms were scraped, and his shirt was ripped and torn. I chuckled inside but did not dare to even give a glimpse of a grin. He had been through enough on his wild ride.

I have a cow whose tag number is 48. She is not mean but has quite an attitude. Most of the time, she is the first to arrive beside my pickup door when I feed a round bale. She then moves to stand about three feet away at the end of my truck, waiting for me to get out to cut the net wrap. She will not let me walk in front of her without jolting me with a headbutt. It started a couple of years ago, and now when my sons-in-law help me feed, they always ask, "Is this the pasture with number 48?" If so, they will only cut the net wrap off the bale from the back of the pickup. Sometimes, I pull out far enough away to completely avoid the cow fight. The next time you drive by one of my corrals and see my pickup and trailer backed up to the end of the alley, just roll down the window and listen. If you hear "You ole rip!" you know that I am somewhere in the middle of all the dust with my sorting stick.

Unlike our cattle, we have the choice to decide which pen we want to be sorted into. The choices we make in this life will decide our future. We are either believers in Christ or unbelievers. In the very end time, we find out about the final roundup in Matthew 25:31–46 (NKJV). It is the parable of the sheep and goats.

> When the Son of Man comes in His glory, and all the holy angels with Him, then He will sit on the throne of His glory. All the nations will be gathered before Him, and He will separate them one from another, as a shepherd divides his sheep from the goats. And He will set the sheep on His right hand, but the goats on the left. Then the King will say to those on His right hand, "Come, you blessed of My Father, inherit the kingdom prepared for you from the foundation of the world: for I was hungry and you gave Me food; I was thirsty and you gave Me drink; I was a stranger and you took Me in; I was naked and you clothed Me; I was sick and you visited Me; I was in prison and you came to Me." Then the righteous will answer Him, saying, "Lord, when did we see You hungry and

feed You, or thirsty and give You drink? When did we see You a stranger and take You in, or naked and clothe You? Or when did we see You sick, or in prison, and come to You?" And the King will answer and say to them, "Assuredly, I say to you, inasmuch as you did it to one of the least of these My brethren, you did it to Me." Then He will also say to those on the left hand, "Depart from Me, you cursed, into the everlasting fire prepared for the devil and his angels: for I was hungry and you gave Me no food; I was thirsty and you gave Me no drink; I was a stranger and you did not take Me in, naked and you did not clothe Me, sick and in prison and you did not visit Me." Then they also will answer Him, saying, "Lord, when did we see You hungry or thirsty or a stranger or naked or sick or in prison, and did not minister to You?" Then He will answer them, saying, "Assuredly, I say to you, inasmuch as you did not do it to one of the least of these, you did not do it to Me." And these will go away into everlasting punishment, but the righteous into eternal life.

CHAPTER 13

Flat Tires

W e all have gotten a flat tire at some point in our lifetime. They never seem to happen at a convenient time, except maybe, when you are home or really close to a tire repair shop. I've had some flat-tire experiences over the years that come to mind. In early September, I was drilling wheat on a Saturday morning when it happened. The local tire repair shop closed at noon, and it was too late for me to take the flat off and get it fixed. So, I had to wait until Monday when they opened again. Another time, as sunrise topped the last hill on my way to start my sixteen-hour day of plowing, I glanced ahead to see my tractor squatting in the field with both rear tires totally flat. Several hours later and $2,000 shorter, my day finally began.

Once, after farming all day, I decided to get a newspaper at Slapout because I wanted to read the sports page. It was already nighttime when I headed out on this four-and-a-half-mile journey. I got my newspaper and was going back home when my rear tire came loose and shot off into a pasture in the dark. I walked the rest of the way home and finally arrived just before midnight. That was the last time I had an urge to buy a newspaper that late in the evening!

I've even had a flat happen while traveling to the local live-stock market pulling a full stock trailer behind my pickup. I heard a loud bang and instantly realized a trailer tire had blown out. The cattle were very restless, and I was not particularly happy about the delay, either. I sat there all alone on the edge of the highway, waiting patiently for my son and daughter-in-law to bring me a spare tire so I could get back on the road. Other times, flats occurred when I didn't have a jack, a lug wrench, or even a spare tire with me. There I sat, stranded, waiting for someone to come by.

Looking back throughout my years, the oddest thing to ever happen to me was when I was headed home on our rural road. I was only a mile from home and had just crossed a small county bridge, traveling at forty-five miles per hour, when a tire passed me on the driver's side. My first reaction was, "Where in the world did that come from?" My question was answered just as quickly with a thump, thump, thump as my hub and axle bounced and dragged along the dirt road. The lug nuts had worked loose and fallen off while the tire and rim raced ahead of me. It finally came to rest in the ditch about 100 feet in front of me.

By now, you get the picture and can relate to the inconvenience of getting a flat. We all have had similar situations that bring us to a complete stop. The tire treads may be worn out, or maybe a rock, nail, or sharp object punctured it. These things just happen. Likewise, as we travel on our highway of life, we can have spiritual flats too. I can recall some personal struggles I have had with spiritual flat tires. These flats are kind of like taking the wrong exit on the highway. This road does not lead to the desired destination, and instead, we get lost. When that happens, it usually takes several more right or left turns until we find the correct road again. We could be distracted by the bright lights over yonder or by the sparkling glitter back there. In either case, our final journey's end has been interrupted and delayed.

In this case, our final destination is heaven. If we do not correct that wrong turn, then we are going to hell—definitely not good! The scriptures found in the Bible are like a road map to help us keep steering in the right direction. The Word of God helps us to know our way and keep us from getting lost. We find in John 14:6 (ESV) where Jesus said, "I am the way, and the truth, and the life. No one comes to the Father except through me."

Spiritual flats might also be caused by old hurt feelings or maybe an old rusty nail that was shaken loose by a bad attitude. It becomes dislodged and works to the surface. These distractions suddenly bring me to a complete halt on my heavenly journey, just like a flat tire on my truck would on the farm. We cannot fix spiritual flats without speaking directly to our Savior. Prayer can get us some road hazard insurance for our spiritual tires. We need this assurance to fix our flat tires and get back out on that road leading to that very special place called heaven.

"I press on toward the goal to win the prize for which God has called me heavenward in Christ Jesus" (Phil. 3:14 NIV).

CHAPTER 14

Muddy Roads

Following the path that stretches ahead of me, I have discovered that it is not always smooth or flat. In fact, some of the roads traveled can become treacherous. Many times, I have stubbed my toe on the rocks that littered the roadway. Living in the country, I always enjoy it when the county dirt roads are freshly graded and free from potholes and washboards. When they are smooth, I can drive faster, without care. Overnight, though, the same roads can become extremely dangerous after a slow, soaking rain, or when several inches of snow have fallen. The first person to drive the next morning has to be very cautious. They tend to drive down the middle of the road. Tire tracks settle in the mud and grooves start to form. The next driver comes along and follows in the same tracks and makes the ruts a little deeper. These ruts, however, form a safety net which prevents other drivers from sliding side to side or getting stuck in a ditch. Over the years, I have found myself in the ditch many times. Most of the time, I get pulled out by a pickup or tractor, but sometimes, I have had to be assisted by the Beaver County road grader operator because I have gotten really hung up in the deep mud. (Assistance from those graders have been more frequent than I would like to admit.)

Our highways can become treacherous with freezing fog, freezing rain, or heavy snow. All of these conditions can cause huge problems. The most dangerous element is freezing mist because the highway appears to be dry even though a hazardous glaze covers it. Once, a slick spot made me do a 360-degree spin. Luckily, my vehicle did not go into the ditch, but I proceeded forward at a much slower and safer speed. Years ago, thick chains were used to pull vehicles to safety, but now, tow ropes are preferred. The bigger around the rope is, the harder the yank is from the other vehicle as it tugs you out of the mess. There is an out-of-control feeling as the vehicle slips and slides with a mind of its own.

The icy and muddy conditions of these roads will always remind me of the times that my spiritual path gets bogged down with some type of rut. These spiritual ruts continue to grow deeper and deeper. Only God can pull me to safety. There are a host of things that cause these spiritual ruts; something as simple as depression, pride, gossip, or envy can eventually lead to getting trapped in these ruts. The only way out is to seek the presence of God and let Him guide you through it. Just like in the natural, the sun will come out and the dark clouds will be rolled away; the path will dry out and become smooth to travel again. May the following scripture help guide you when the road gets bumpy and things begin to speed out of control. In Hebrews 12:1 (NIV), it is written: "Therefore, since we are surrounded by such a great cloud of witnesses, let us throw off everything that hinders and the sin that so easily entangles. And let us run with perseverance the race marked out for us."

CHAPTER 15

Casting Stones

My daughter-in-law, Rachael, and son, Ryan, purchased the property next to their house. Since it had two irrigation pivots on it, they chose to plant alfalfa in both circles. Much work had to be done to prepare the ground for this particular crop. The soil needed to be smooth and firm for the seedbed. The south circle consisted of eighty acres. Fifteen of those were on a sand hill that was scattered with rocks.

They had planted the crop the previous August, and the young plants had sprouted with repeated watering from their irrigation system. The plants began to grow into late fall, right before they went dormant through the winter months. Now that spring was here, the alfalfa stand was firmly established. Just one problem remained, however. The bigger rocks had to be removed before the hay season started in the summer. If not, the rocks would interfere with or damage the equipment used to swathe and bale the alfalfa hay.

Unfortunately, the only way to pick up the multitude of rocks was by hand. To the great surprise of both of my daughters and their families, we would commence this activity during their spring breaks. The day before my daughter Kareece and her two sons, Kade and Tyce, were to arrive, we started this task. Rachael, Ryan, Justin, Charlene, and I were armed with twelve five-gallon buckets. We placed them about thirty feet apart on the field and began the difficult task of bending over and picking up rocks one by one and tossing them into the buckets. We repeatedly dumped our full buckets into the front-end loader of our small John Deere tractor. After two hours of work, we realized this job was going to become a rather huge undertaking. We took a long break then continued picking up rocks in the evening for two more hours.

What started as kind of fun and exciting soon became a major challenge. The next morning, our hamstrings screamed with each step we took. None of us could express just how much we were hurting because Kareece and her two sons were eager to join our work. They were so invigorated that beautiful cool morning in the fresh country air. They hustled and nearly sprinted from rock to rock while the rest of us moved slowly and went through the motions, battling constant, sharp pain. We did fairly well in concealing the depth of our hurt by constantly smiling and chatting with our new team members. They too were extremely sore the next morning.

Two days later, my youngest daughter, Janée, and her husband, Dan, and their two children, Brynna and Aidan, joined the fray. Nobody was about to drop any hints about the upcoming pain they would experience. We did not say a word as we let them set the pace. They were real troopers as they picked up rocks at record speed. The next morning was really ugly. Our house was full of moaning and groaning as soon as their feet hit the floor, and the pungent smell of muscle ointment lingered throughout the day. It was good that they helped us finish our last day. Both daughters and all my grandchildren let it be known that they would never, ever help pick up rocks again in *any* field. By the tone in their stern voices, I think that they really meant what they were saying. When it was all said and done, we removed somewhere around 15,000 rocks during that spring break.

Long before the agonizing "Easter Egg Rock Hunt," my grandchildren were avid rock hounds whenever they visited the farm. Our excursions took us to gravel pits, creek bottoms, and exposed sides of the hills in our pastures. Each one gathered their favorites and brought them home to wash and sort. Their moms determined how many they could take home. These memories of seeing the excitement on their faces as they chose their favorites brought me untold pleasure.

Spending time with my little rock hounds, along with our family-bonding experience in the alfalfa field, reminded me of a scripture that helps in my spiritual walk. John 8:6–11 (NASB) says,

> They were saying this, testing Him, so that they might have grounds for accusing Him. But Jesus stooped down and with His finger wrote on the ground. But when they persisted in asking Him, He straightened up, and said to them, "He who is without sin among you, let him be the first to throw a stone at her." Again, He stooped down and wrote on the ground. When they heard it, they began to go out one by one, beginning with the older ones, and He was left alone, and the woman, where she was, in the center of the court. Straightening up, Jesus said to her, "Woman, where are they? Did no one condemn you?" She said, "No one, Lord." And Jesus said,

"I do not condemn you, either. Go. From now
on sin no more."

These scriptures speak volumes. They tell me to be very careful of any stone that I'm about to cast. It is best to simply lay it back down gently. I have sorted through many rocks, and in doing so, I found my favorite. It is a spiritual one found in Psalm 18:2. It reads, "The Lord is my rock, and my fortress, and my deliverer; my God, my strength, in whom I will trust; my buckler, and the horn of my salvation, and my high tower."

CHAPTER 16

The Potter and That Lump of Clay

Glancing back at the past seventy years of cultivating the land on our family farm, I have compiled some calculations from the decades I have spent tilling the soil. I started driving the tractor at the age of thirteen and pulled behind it a one-way plow, a sweep, an offset disc, harrows, grain-planting drills, or a chisel. I figure that over the last fifty-seven years of pulling these implements, I have plowed over 150,000 acres, refilled the tractor fuel tanks with either gas, propane, or diesel over 3,000 times, used over 100,000 gallons of diesel, and sat on the tractor seat for over 25,000 hours. I have spent countless hours watching and counting hawks flying lazily in the sky, even witnessing forty at one time. I've also watched them perch on fenceposts, ready to pounce at any sign of movement as they search for their prey of field mice and rats. I have drunk several thousand cups of coffee from my thermos and lost count of the number of water bottles I've taken from my cooler. In my younger years, we used gallon glass jugs wrapped with soaked burlap rags which were secured with wire to ensure the drinking water stayed cool a little longer.

The years have brought numerous flat tires, breakdowns, lightning strikes, soaking rains, and gusty winds that stirred up lots of blowing dust. I've seen it all! Tractors with no cabs, some with umbrellas, and later others with air-conditioners that sometimes worked and at other times did not. My work days have varied from just a few hours to some that lasted eighteen hours and more. My time spent alone often consisted of merely thinking, listening to music or to the cattle and grain market updates, and praying for my fellow neighbors. Of course, I am always ready and eager to wave hello to any passerby that might drive by on these lonely, dusty roads.

These long hours in the field have brought some very challenging times as well. Many times, disc bearings would wear out on the offset disc plow. It was a chore to replace these bearings, and I would be covered with dirt and grease from head to toe. This happened many times throughout the years. Probably the thing that I hated the most was stopping the tractor to clean out the buildup of dirt and straw on the plow, usually caused by gourd vines or goat head stickers. The sweep plow had these beams called frogs that dropped down from the frame and attached to the sweep blades. Any weeds that had vines that spread out on the ground would wrap around each frog and cause deep furrows in the ground. Backing up the tractor didn't help remove them; the only way to get them off was to dig out all the buildup by hand. It was certainly not an easy thing to do; nevertheless, it had to be done. Countless times over the years, I was down on both hands and knees unwrapping these vines away from the frogs.

In order to prepare the fields for alfalfa seed planting, it is necessary to make them smooth by pulling a small harrow many times over the fields at different angles to break up the dirt clods. You have to be very careful not to turn the small tractor too sharply to change directions. One of the cables hooked to the harrow could catch on the back tractor tire, and it would pull the harrow upward toward you. My mom loved to drive the tractor and would help out once in a while. I remember the brand-new barbed wire fence that my neighbor and I had just completed with tightly stretched wire and new t-posts driven perfectly in a straight row. Mom came to relieve me during the noon hour while I ate. She made that first round, heading west, without looking back to see where the sweep plow was. She got too close to the fence and clipped about twelve posts and bent them over. As she got off the tractor, she said, "I must have gotten a little close to the fence." I couldn't say a word because I have done the same thing.

Once my dad tried to help me out and decided he would start drilling wheat at the house. Drilling wheat consists of pulling two fourteen-foot grain drills together, making for a twenty-eight-foot swath. He was not used to drilling because that had been my job for over thirty years. But he was really good at sweeping the fields. On his first round, the drills swung out too far, and he got the outside drill wheel caught on a new irrigation pivot being installed. He cratered one of the wheels on the pivot in addition to doing extensive damage to the drill by wedging it underneath the pivot. I was on my way home, and as I was crossing the bridge, I could see what looked to be a major wreck from half a mile away. The drills were setting at odd angles underneath the pivot. I immediately went to see what had happened. He was very frustrated, but I didn't say anything because I had gotten the drills into tight situations before too.

There is a very unique smell to a freshly plowed field that cannot be found elsewhere. The best way to describe it is that of a rich, heavy, musty aroma. In the soil, there is a certain type of bacteria which produces an organic chemical called geosmin. When the ground is plowed, it causes a chemical reaction that produces this pleasant smell; it is not the dirt itself. My farm ground consists of several types of soil: I have sandy acres, some loamy acres, and some clay acres. These soil types are very different from each other. The sandy soil is poor and lightweight. This soil is lacking in nutrients that the plants need to grow. It produces low yields of wheat production, but since it has less crop residue, this soil is easy to till.

The loamy acres have the ability to retain moisture and nutrients. This makes them much more suitable for farming and raising crops. Loam is a medium-textured soil that stores the most organic matter in it, allowing for the best yields of wheat grain at harvest time. I also have clay soil, which is tightly compacted. This makes it very difficult for the moisture and air to penetrate. It can prevent plants' roots from taking hold properly and can even stunt their growth. This heavy, dense soil tends to store water and not drain well.

A parable found in the Bible in Matthew 13:18–23 tells us about the story of the sower. Sometimes the seed is sown and then blown by the wayside. Or, it may be sown into stony places which does not take root and endures for only a while. Perhaps, it is sown among the thorns and is soon choked out. However, if it is sown in good ground, it will produce and bear fruit. It will bring forth a harvest, either thirty, sixty, or a hundredfold.

This speaks to me as a farmer who sows seeds. It is very important to have the ground prepared properly to plant the seed for that bountiful harvest, which applies not only for our crops, but spiritually as well. The rich loam soil, full of nutrients and life, is easy to cultivate after the harvest. The sandy soil is easy to cultivate too. But, tilling up clay soil is a different matter altogether. When clay is too wet, the sweep plow and off-set disc tend to get plugged up with mud. When the clay soil is too dry, the implements cannot penetrate the hard ground. Thinking about the spiritual realm, perhaps I may have been more like the clay at times. Romans 9:21 says, "Hath not the potter power over the clay, of the same lump to make one vessel unto honor, and another unto dishonor?" God has sovereignty over His creation in the heavens and on the earth. If we choose to seek Him, God will transform us through His salvation and mercy to be followers in His kingdom. I can look back now and see the many challenges the Master Potter had in molding me into something useful from that hardened lump of clay. The potter had to use every implement that I have ever used in my farm operation to mold me into a vessel of honor for His kingdom. I say to you today that I have sinned, but our Father in heaven died on the cross and because I have confessed all my sins, I have been forgiven. I have overcome the flesh and the devil by the blood of Jesus and by the word of my testimony. Hallelujah!

CHAPTER 17

Three Strikes

I t was a Saturday evening worship service in mid-July of 2014 on the banks of the Kiowa Creek in eastern Beaver County. Several of us had gathered to listen to the founder of Speak His Word Ministries, Gail Winter, who is a gifted author and renowned speaker. Sitting in my lawn chair under the shade of a huge elm tree, I listened to live Christian music on the pleasant, cool evening. A light, southerly breeze ushered in the sweet aroma of sagebrush. The rustling sound of leaves and branches as they swayed back-and-forth filled the background. Just a few feet away from me, crystal blue water flowed gently down the stream. The ripple effects of the water as it moved across the rocks that rested on the river bed was a pleasant sound to hear. White, fluffy storm clouds repeatedly tried to form, but to no avail, as a host of angels kept them at bay all evening long. This scene perfectly captured the harmony of peace and calm that filled the evening air.

With eyes closed, my mind turned back to a vision that I had received only a few months earlier. As I recalled it, the Holy Spirit surrounded me with His presence and revealed the

93

true meaning of my vision. First, let me share the vision with you. In it, I was playing baseball on a dry, dusty lot. The wind gusts kept the dust churned up on the infield the entire game. I was standing in the batter's box, digging in, ready to face the opposing pitcher. The first pitch, a fastball, sailed toward the plate. I swung mightily and missed. I stepped out of the batter's box, wiped my eyes, swished my tongue against the grit on my teeth. Then, I stepped back into the box to wait for the next pitch. The pitcher reached back, and with everything he had, he cut loose and launched another fastball that raced toward home plate. Again, I swung and missed. Now down with an 0–2 count, I shortened my grip, determined and focused to get a hit. The pitcher wound up and delivered another fastball that zoomed toward me. This time, I barely got a piece of the ball with the end of my bat for a foul tip. The catcher reached to snag it, but the ball popped out of his mitt. Had he caught the ball, it would have been strike three for me. I would have been out of the game, but now, I got another chance at bat.

Then the scene changed dramatically. I was still standing in the batter's box, waiting for the final pitch, but now, instead of being in the dusty field, I could see thousands of fans filling a huge stadium. They were all there to watch me play. The pitcher glared at the catcher from the pitcher's mound, where he stood tall, waiting to pick up the catcher's sign. This time, his pitch seemed to dance as it rushed straight toward the middle of the plate. I swung with all my might, and this time, I connected with the ball. It jumped off my bat and sailed high toward the centerfield fence and continued over it for a homerun. As I circled the bases, the crowd came to their feet, cheering for me and the towering homerun I had just hit.

Now, back to the evening service in July. With my eyes still closed, my Father in heaven revealed the meaning of the vision to me. The first strike was the cancer in my left kidney. The second strike was cancer in my lungs. The third strike represented brain cancer. The foul tip allowed me another chance to live and gave me the opportunity to find His purpose for me in the remaining years of my life. When I opened my eyes, I saw the sagebrush branches waving in the wind on both sides of the creek. They represented the huge crowd of people standing and cheering me on. The trees in the far distance, at that moment, represented the centerfield fence. I want to thank Gail Winter for that special July summer night service on the banks of the Kiowa Creek. It was anointed.

CHAPTER 18

Drinking from My Saucer

This poem by John Paul Moore sums up where my life stands today. I have witnessed dark clouds and had to wait until the sun's rays pushed through them. We all choose how to live this life and all that it brings with it. Yes, we will face setbacks, but we will come back stronger than ever before. This life has brought me many blessings. Today, I tell you, it feels awesome to drink from my saucer because my cup has overflowed. After tasting that first sip, you suddenly realize that the blessings will continue to flow. They are multiplied many times over as you continue to drink from that precious saucer. To witness a smile on the face of a stranger that needed a little help that day. Or maybe just a simple note to the hotel maid after your stay along with a great tip, *"Thanks for the clean room. My room was excellent! Hope you have a blessed day."* It doesn't take much effort at all to show respect for others.

Several artists have sung powerful versions of this poem, "Drinking from the Saucer," that helped encourage me greatly on my journey. I have truly enjoyed the small things in life these past ten years.

Drinking from the Saucer

By John Paul Moore

I have never made a fortune,
And I will never make one now.
But it really doesn't matter
Because I am happy anyhow.

As I go along my journey,
I am reaping better than I've sowed.
I am drinking from the saucer
Because my cup has overflowed.

I don't have a lot of riches,
And sometimes the going's tough.
But with kin and friends to love me,
I think I am rich enough.

I thank God for the blessings
That His mercy has bestowed.
I'm drinking from the saucer
Because my cup has overflowed.

He gives me strength and courage
When the way grows steep and rough.
I will not ask for other blessings, for
I am already blessed enough.

May we never be too busy
To help bear another's load.

Then we will all be drinking from the saucer
When our cups have overflowed.

Used with permission from the author's family

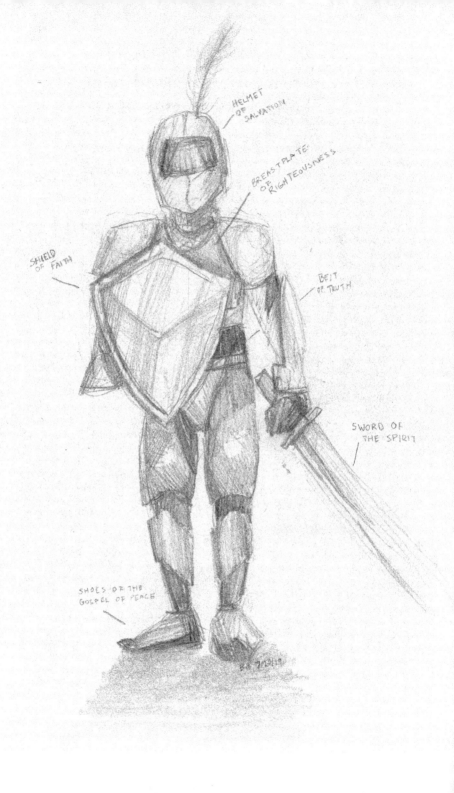

HELMET
OF SALVATION

BREASTPLATE
OF
RIGHTEOUSNESS

SHIELD
OF FAITH

BELT
OF TRUTH

SWORD OF
THE SPIRIT

SHOES OF THE
GOSPEL OF PEACE

CHAPTER 19

Fearless Warrior

W e will all face trials and tribulations on our journey. These obstacles will present very real hurdles and roadblocks that often seem impossible to navigate. But, from reading His words in the Bible, we learn that when we suit up with God's armor, we are equipped to fight any battle. Our full protection includes the shield of faith, the helmet of salvation, the sword of the Spirit, the breastplate of righteousness, truth that girds our loins, and the gospel of eternal peace that encases our feet. Always cling to that hope living deep within our souls. It does not matter how fierce the winds are, how dark the clouds get, nor the fury of the storm that hovers, waiting to engulf us. What matters is that on the other shore, we can see glimpses of sunlight shining brightly.

Many warriors lined up and joined forces to help me on that epic battlefield where I fought stage IV kidney cancer that had spread to my lungs and brain. I grabbed onto those promises of hope that these warriors surrounded me with daily. They provided incredible words of encouragement, uplifting phone calls, and countless texts containing scriptures and words of life.

Now healed, I have renewed hope to complete the mission that lies before me. Today, I can honestly stand before you and say from the bottom of my heart that many of my greatest blessings have come during the most troubling of times. My last words to all those warriors out there: Thank you so much for standing tall with me. My wishes are that when my trail has come to the end, my ashes will be spread on my favorite hill overlooking the valley below. Stake a small wooden cross there with the inscription that reads, "*Fearless Warrior.*"

"And we know that all things work together for good to them that love God, to them who are the called according to His purpose" (Romans 8:28).

CHAPTER 20

Soooo Long, Farewell

Thanks for allowing me the time to share these three visions with you along with a few short stories of my life experiences. Each chapter is a vivid reminder of just how much our Father in heaven loved and comforted me along the way.

To each one of you, my hope and prayer is that you find peace and tranquility in your special place of refuge and solace. My refuge lies in that small valley between the banks of the Indian and Kiowa Creeks, that surreal strip of fertile land that once was home to Indian tribes and roaming buffalo.

To those of you whom I have not met and to some of you that I may not see again, my prayer is that God's grace covers you always and brings you comfort. To those out there whose paths will likely cross with mine again, my prayer is for God's blessings to continue to pour down upon you.

We will all face obstacles along the way. There will be times when our hearts will be very troubled, and other times when our hearts will be full of joy. It's so important not to dwell on our faults and mistakes, but rather focus our minds on better things to come. At the end of the day when evening has come, everything that has happened will fade away into yesterday and will soon be forgotten.

Live each moment of every day to the fullest and never wish for tomorrow. For what we have is today. Enjoy it to the fullest and strive to make each moment the very best possible. Be fully prepared to lend a hand to help others when an opportunity arises. We will have struggles from time to time, but I believe that we were all born to be overcomers and that God's Word will stand forever. Just one last scripture to share before we part ways. We must always remember that no matter how great the odds seem, our Awesome God is right there walking along beside us each step of the way, and He will never forsake us. Rejoice and be joyful to the Lord. In the book of Romans 15:5–6 (ESV), it reads, "May the God of endurance and encouragement grant you to live in such harmony with one another, in accord with Christ Jesus, that together you may with one voice glorify the God and Father of our Lord Jesus Christ."

I look forward to sharing my testimony in person too. God has added an extra chapter to my life. I would be happy to share about His grace in the surrounding areas with a church, a Sunday school class, a youth activity, a school classroom, at a coffee shop, or even on a street corner. You can reach me at kcfarmsslapout@gmail.com. I look forward to hearing from you.

Special Thanks

Conservation has always been a huge part of my life. I have served many years on the Beaver County Conservation Board and would like to thank and congratulate the Secretaries, the Equipment Mangers, and the District Directors. Your commitment and dedication to conservation has been outstanding. Thank you for the excellent work that you do at the district level across this great state.

As I approach the ten-year mark of serving as Area 1 Commissioner for the Oklahoma Conservation Commission, I can say that many great things have happened in conservation in our outstanding state. To the leadership of the officer team in OACD, for the planning of not only the state and area meetings each year, but also in keeping all the districts updated with the latest information—I say a job well done. A great big thanks to our awesome state staff in Administration, AML, Conservation Programs, District Services, Geographic Information and Technical Service, Water Quality, Blue Thumb Education, Soil Health, Watershed Projects, Water Quality Monitoring, and Wetlands. You all are truly amazing. To our friends in NRCS who team up with conservation to form an outstanding partnership, I really appreciate all of you as we accomplish even greater goals working together. It has been a pleasure to have worked with such outstanding Executive and Assistant Executive Directors. Each of you set very high standards by your work ethic. Lastly, to my fellow Commissioners, it has been an honor to serve alongside each of you. Thanks for all the time spent and dedication in serving this cause for our land, our heritage, our future. To my Conservation family at both the district and state level, you have brought me many fond memories that I will cherish the rest of my life. I treasure each one of you and the friendships that we have created.

About the Author

Hi, my name is Karl Jett, son of Delvin and Ramona Jett. Growing up on the family farm in the Oklahoma Panhandle, I always knew that I wanted to be a farmer too. I had the opportunity to come back to the farm and partner with my dad after college. I majored in Agriculture Economics at Oklahoma State University and graduated in 1972. During college, I married my high school sweetheart, Charlene Bowers. Our first child was born in Stillwater, and we named her Cherinda. Our family grew with the addition of another daughter, Kareece, a couple of years later. A few years after her birth, another daughter, Janée, joined our family, followed by the birth of our son, Ryan.

My time spent on the farm consisted of farming wheat, raising alfalfa, and managing a cow-calf operation. Our kids were all involved with FFA and 4-H activities, along with showing cattle, sheep, and hogs during their years at Laverne School. In addition to their show animal projects, they participated in track, basketball, baseball, and football. Our Sundays were spent with our awesome church family at the Fairview United Methodist Church near Slapout. Now, with my children all grown up, Charlene and I have been blessed with five wonderful grandchildren.

I am a fourth-generation farmer-rancher who is passionate about conserving our natural resources and protecting our land for future generations. I have served many years on the Beaver County Conservation Board, and for the last ten years, I have served as Area 1 Commissioner for the State of Oklahoma Conservation Commission.